JAYDN

Out, Voyage

BROKEN SLEEP BOOKS

Published 2020,
Broken Sleep Books:
Cornwall / Wales

brokensleepbooks.com

First Edition

Lay out your unrest.

Publisher/Editor: Aaron Kent
Editor: Charlie Baylis

Typeset in UK by Aaron Kent

Broken Sleep Books is committed to
a sustainable future for our planet,
and therefore uses print on
demand publication.

brokensleepbooks@gmail.com

ISBN: 9781660024209

Contents

How do you rehearse the unknown?
—Wayne Shorter

Out, Voyage

Jaydn DeWald

Arrangement, Nuclear

We discovered our house was spheroid, like the earth.

Our beds were afloat on moonlit carpets.

Our daughter feverishly drawing circles in black crayon on butcher paper—did she think she was stirring a potion, generating a storm?

I used to write poems ending with lone boats creaking at sundown.

All winter we perched on stools in our garage, piecing together scorched-edged shreds of a map.

Our son gently pulled our eyelashes, or he squirmed his hands inside our mouths as though we were sock puppets.

Suddenly a dark wave of laundry crashed over us.

I closed my eyes, I listened to womb noises, I tasted burnt toast in the air.

Like the earth, too, our house was rotating.

My partner wore a long sheer nightgown that she swished around and around until she disappeared—

Sonnet Granadas

for Bill Evans

Six chords, then silence, then the world
  Was made. Just like my heart in its feeble
Birdcage. It was autumn. I listened with
  Eyes closed. Light strobing among leaves,

The phonograph crackling and popping
  As if your *Trio with Symphony Orchestra*
Was burning, Bill, right in the fireplace.

  Stone angel, little deep-thinking statuette—
I was the dragonfly lighted in your hair,
  I was the moss around your demure ankle.

A huddle of grass shivering as if afraid.
  Tell me, Bill. How did you do all of that?
How'd you make the yellow leaves fall,
  The pond, in slow motion, ripple inward?

Past Developing

Forget the waitress who resembled Sappho.
The salt cod she served us drifted like sand
Between the tines of our forks. On the tube
Sat children painting little clay St. Jeromes,
But even that light made her cheeks glisten.
"I'm greener than the grass is green," I said,
And raised the centuries-old wine that had
Our heads spinning. I dreamt of the Gorilla
Suit I wore in college—the darkness inside.
Behind the bar stood the rotted, black mast
To which Odysseus had been tied. And yet
Its placard: *None of this is being preserved*
Via video surveillance. Our hunk of peasant
Bread. Those paper placemats. Plates of oil.
We carried around our necks huge Polaroid
Cameras, so there was no use remembering.
Through red window curtains, light caught
Us red-handed, napkins rising to our noses.
On the specials chalkboard, the old barman
Playing Hangman. One leg. No I's. No face.

Acting, Method

Once, on stage, a boy became
    My Father. I knelt before him
And he placed two fish bones

On my tongue. Rank, delicate
    Little bones. Our blue skyline

Rustled. Two choirboys, each
    On a white cloud, rode by me
Laughing & jerking overhead.

It was a beautiful age to learn
    Pain. One could walk, sunsets,

In orange pastures, venting to
    One's boring donkey. Gazing
So often into the black mouth

Of a well—one was forced to
    Consider Death. Three priests

Started (stage left) to feed me
    Lines: *His body is home now.*
His body is at home, I said &

Munched those little bones to
    Sand. My Father stared down

Repulsed or stunned or afraid.
    In rolled a backdrop of purple
Mountains. Then a single girl

In a red tutu, spinning around
    Like a small, overzealous fire.

The Hammock

My neighbor hung a hammock   from the porch
Of his solid glass mansion,   so that whenever a sleepy passerby
Decided to snooze there   (it was late October, & yellow
Orange red updrafts of leaves   —miniature tornados—
Would appear to entrance folks   & lead them
Straight toward it)   he could strut   buck naked across the transparent
Floor overhead,   enticing her or him   to come upstairs.
Just yesterday,   watching from my study window
Across the street, I was nearly   enticed to wander over there
Myself—I'd already   buttoned to the throat   my red
Flannel mackinaw—   when I saw a woman thinly reflected
In glass   all around her, circling   his hammock the way
One might circle   a small Italian sports car. Meanwhile,
My neighbor approached her   as soundless as a spider
From above . . .   Gradually, ungripping my lace curtain,
I saw that the woman   was dressed like me—stone-

washed jeans & sneakers & the red   flannel mackinaw — as though
She were my reflection & it was I   circling the hammock
Running two fingers   along its crisply folded edge. Resolved
To go out there, to be at last   with my reflections, I started
Toward the door,   though scarcely had I taken half a step
When a shrill yowl   exploded from without,   & I spun
Back to the window: there,   above the hammock, above
My doppelgänger's head,   a peacock with fanned
Iridescent plumage   yowled & strutted in a tight semi-   circle,
& again yowled & strutted & then   yowled again; & the woman,
In response, raised her hands   palm outward   & slowly
Backed down the porch . . .   Already
I was lumbering out my door,   never mind that my neighbor
Had disappeared or else   metamorphosed into a peacock. Already
I was in the center of my lawn,   slashing my bare hands
Through a tornado   of red orange yellow leaves that—
Like the static rustling   of a TV—   blotted out
His entire mansion. Then   just as swiftly darkness fell, the leaves
Settled at my feet, & I stood there   at the border
Of our adjoined yards   as though I was still at my window, still
A mere shadow   behind pink lace. I gazed up

At my neighbor's porch   now thronged with uniformed
Police officers (& their   reflections) strobing eerily
    Red & blue, no   sound at all, in their cruisers'
Lightbars. Five or six of them   rushed toward me: I didn't—
    Couldn't—move. Roughly   I was lifted into the air & conveyed,
Crowd-surf-style,   onto the porch, where five or six others
    Hip-   thrusting to music I could only   now hear thumping
Faintly beyond the glass walls   commenced to tug
    At the sleeves   of my mackinaw & to untuck
My lime green   button-up. In seconds   they had me shirt-
    less, & were about to   start in (to my very literal   *Stop!*
Excitement) on my jeans,   when a voice barked:
    & onto the porch   strode my neighbor, buck naked,
Smeared with their watery   red-&-blues. I stepped   backward; I saw
    Myself—or was it   another doppelgänger?—in the reflection
In the glass, sprinting   up the street,   just as the woman had,
    Though I remained   on the porch, sensing the hammock
Behind me the way one   might sense
    A hole in the earth. *Is it mystery,   the unknown, you are after?*
Asked my neighbor,   backing me up
    Against the hammock.   *Sexual transcendence?* He tilted his head

Questioningly. *Love?* Some-   body had unzipped
          My jeans, which now slid   to my ankles: I almost tripped.
Yes, I said. *All   of those things. Yes.* Where-
          upon he slipped   from his dense   thatch of pubic hair
A long   iridescent peacock feather & at once
          Brushed it—its turquoise eye   stared at me—in wide arcs
Across my chest, as though tracing   a symbol. Then:
          You too must sleep, he said. Meaning   the world
Isn't good enough.   *Don't worry—   I'll wake you.*
          I'll wake   all of you, I heard him say   as I fell back
Into the hammock, fell back   into the feathered
Darkness   of sleep & am still   falling . . .

14

Round Midnight

i lie
   sleepless

for a few
   minutes

then return
   to my partner

washing
   my face

in a huge pail
   of water

on which
   the red moon

sparkles
   down her

white
   forearms

but i know
   i am sleeping

i can hear
   outside

my tent
   the white-

tailed fawn
   rolling

my ripe
  cantaloupe

with her
  black muzzle

toward her
  warm place

in the leaves
  & needles

Voyage Out

He's standing beside his hammock, above his sleeping body, which dreams of stumbling along an ever-winding path of leaves & ashes, when a distant, quavering soprano begins to sing—a voice he'd heard, years before, on a bronze hill overlooking the ocean, & ever since regretted not searching for, not hurtling toward her in the rubescent dusk of summer, tearing off his rucksack. "Wake up," he tells his body, nudging its shoulder with his knee. But it goes on lying there, an enormous baby in a sling, because it is dying in its sleep: it has collapsed on the dark path among the scraping leaves, watching his twelve-year-old daughter in her plum-black dress (so like a dream within a dream) stumble forward in its place. He runs his hand over the blond hairs of its forearm. Then he stares up at the white light through the lemon trees & at his daughter dancing, one rainy evening, before the old projector, the old faces of relatives (contorted, celery-green) streaked across her flannel PJs. What can account for this desire to hurtle out into the streets, to find the soprano's voice, rising again, in the paling distance? *Art thou a little spirit bearing up a corpse*, as Epictetus said, or is the soprano tempting him—like an egret on a thin branch—to leave, to let the body go? His daughter, at the beach with some friends, in the tarantualic shadow of a palm tree, will no doubt walk, hours later, over the damp grass toward his body, then suddenly freeze in the middle of the yard—warm & windless & the moon in her salt-hardened hair—noticing a smudge of white, the peak of his nose, above the hammock. Now he's touching for the last time (as his daughter will, crumpling to her knees) the paper eyelids, the colorless lips & ill-shaven chin. O how he's dreamt of the soprano silhouetted on an ice floe, of lurching toward her through rags of swirling snow, burning to see her, to watch her sing! Soon his daughter, as she replaced his body in its dream, will be standing right here in this place before the hammock, trying again & again to shape these wooden fingers around her tiny hand—although by then, of course, he will be long gone, loping across violet sands, searching for the soprano: the quavering voice, the painted mouth . . .

Triad

I am sequestered in the greenhouse again, pensive,
    Snipping little branches. He (my son) has no need

    To search for me, as he used to. See? His window
Is open; he is practicing Schumann, *Kinderszenen,*

Op. 15, a way of calling to me. But I won't budge.
    She may be with him, like a terrible nun / gripping

A black stick. Hah—if that were true, I would not
    Have left the chicken, beheaded, in the white sink

    To cower among marigolds. Her stupid / naïveté
Terrifies me: at any moment, I feel she may utter:

    I love your father. Or, worse: *We love each other.*
    Thus the shears trembling in my pale hands. Thus

I could snip my manhood. Beyond the glass walls,
    Light caught in the bare tree; my son approaching

    The fourth piece, "Pleading Child," with his green
Drapes billowing. I feel I shouldn't be / permitted

    Such beauty. My gorged flowers hang their heads.
    Son: I want you to hear how Horowitz played this

In Hamburg, June, 1987—the album's by my bed—
    But shame, like a horrendous crashing of the keys,

    Stoops me forward. Here, tormented, I will remain.
I am your father, I can never / allow myself to heal.

Landscape with Sashimi

Yoshi's Jazz Club & Japanese Restaurant
— San Francisco, April 2008

his birthday   he's drunk   he keeps

ramming his bell against the mic   still

he tries to scream   to shred   I mean

to simply tear it up, man   like he did

on *First Light*   1971   with Hancock

Henderson   Carter   Benson

DeJohnette & so on   but he's

a different player   a different person

now   his solo   a flock of ungainly

tin birds scattering pell-mell   he can

only stand there grumbling   fiddling

with his valves   after a few measures

of nothing   Hutcherson bursts in

four-malleted   open-mouthed   &

Freddie whips around   as though to

make him listen   respectful   head

bowed   should I storm out   hop in

my olive-green Saab   blast *Hub-Tones*

& forget it all   the whole evening

the audience hollering   *Red Clay! Little*

Sunflower!   Yesterday's Dreams!   Well

there he is   the Hub of Hubbard

slumped on his stool   defeated   one

hand fondling the fat   pink child

of his underlip Oh   come on, Freddie

give it up   we forgive   your drinking

your chops   even your hubris   still

know this   I will not be the one white

strait-   laced person   who tries to

describe your prowess   to the poor

young   oblivious waitress   leaning

over my table   handing me my dish of

lugubrious   *uni*

Sleeping Lions

the willing giving over of the self to the other, to power
—Jack Halberstam

When I arrived, around noon, at the Blue Danube Café,
    A plump gentleman clambered up out of his pink chair
Begging me to take his seat, please, sit down, sit down.
    My feet tingled. "Splendid," I said. Another large man
Began to take my arms out of my coat. "Ahead of time,
    As usual," said a petite woman, seated across from me,
Lifting her demitasse. She seemed to resemble a figure
    From my deepest past. A hand was placed on my knee.
A pale hand on my dark trousers. A girl, in front of me,
    Asking me what I should like to order. "Coffee, strong,"
I said. A faint, meaningful light haunted the blank wall
    Behind the counter. A woman beside the petite woman
Said: "Oh, dear, you must be tired," and, indeed, I was

Half asleep. My mother hung above me, tucking me in,
    Pulling the white sheet up over my face. "I'm fatigued,"
I told the woman, though she had long since moved on
    To wittier conversation. "How ambitious he used to be,"
Said a young chap staring down at me. "What a waste,"
    His friend agreed. In a circular mirror, on the side wall,
The whitest snow fell. My porcelain cup of cold coffee
    Sloshed about in my lap as if I was driving somewhere
To the din of battle drums. Still, I was courteously still.
    "He seems, well, *excited*," said a tanned young woman,
Coming right up to my face. A couple of bookish boys
    Stood watching. "I wouldn't do that," one of them said,
Grimacing. "No," said the other. "I think that's enough."

Little Boxes

Lost woman of Lilliput,
the witness, midwife to my agonies,

raised to the heavens,
most phlegmatic of mates,

I have trapped you
in one of Popa's little boxes—

but you only sit there crosslegged,
nibbling your fingernails,

a shoebox painted black
and purfled with many cottonballs.

stroking your tow-colored hair.
In the meantime, I am crouched

How lonesome it must be
to stand there all alone, to do nothing

in my ill-lit basement with one eye
narrowed in your moonhole,

but stare at this endless four-sided night . . .
With a butcher's knife,

listening to my wife's continuous
clopping footfalls overhead . . .

I poke tiny holes for stars, a larger hole
for my blinkless eye—the moon.

Then I stand an Army Man inside,
the one whose rifle is forever

"Just one more little box," I say,
among an infinity of little boxes,

handing you one, which happens to be
coffin-shaped and just your size.

The Domesticated Troubadour

he's too young for it now   the romantic posturing
on rain-   soaked terraces   & the distant sea
crashing   his kids are putting   clips in his hair
outer-space stickers   on his sunburst strat
now it's more than enough   to leap from cushion
to matte-gray cushion   avoiding carpet-lava
& calling for help across   minute distances   even when
he hauls out the garbage   past midnight   odor
of damp leaves in darkness   there is no inkling
of song in him   he's sure the romance will return
someday   in a sweep of cheatgrass   cloud-
shadows drifting   over his open palms   but then
where will his kids be   when again will he count
with eyes closed   or rise from among their sleeping
bodies   so quietly   he almost forgets
his ancient calling   almost forgets   to breathe

Voyage Out (2)

My sister's creative, more than creative than I, though less creative than my brother, whose creativity I sometimes believe must be an act. Just this morning, for example, I watched him slip into his backpack the C- English paper he'd hung by a length of string from our carport all semester, planning to turn it in, he told me, now that it was browned and wrinkled and torn in places, like three treasure maps stapled together, as a "rewrite." And yet my sister, whose creativity I never question, is no doubt the likelier *poseur*, being a charter member of the Cinemaniacs (a club that watches and squabbles over films) and herself an impassioned method actor. Once, for a whole month, she floated from room to room in a peach-colored maiden's gown, speaking to invisible interlocutors in an angelic, barely audible British accent. Well, maybe they're both acting—they're teenagers. You can imagine, I'm sure, how difficult it is to live with them; too much creativity can be a liability: not every occasion calls for shoving a black fishnet stocking into the horn of our old Victrola, even if it does make Prokofiev sound a bit naughtier. Tonight, like every night for the last month, I have plopped down on our brown leather sofa (afghan draped around my shoulders, bowl of movie-butter popcorn in my lap) to watch reruns—the most un- or anti-creative thing I can imagine. All the time I feel my sister and brother stare down at me from the landing of our staircase, as though from a rain-soaked dock, while I unmoor my little sofa-shaped boat. They are, I am certain, waiting for some long-overdue creative outpouring. Why else would they be so quiet? *Fine. Let them sigh*, I tell myself. *Let them grip the banister, let them whisper vulturously among themselves.* Having no more use for creativity than for, say, an encyclopedia of modern chess openings, I now simply let myself drift away into the make-believe mist over the make-believe water, sockfeet propped on our leather cushions, chuckling to an episode of *M*A*S*H*.

Acting, Method (2)

In Cork, Ireland, I stopped at this little cottage-like restaurant
    And there sat Homer, all alone, hunkered over a bowl of stew.

I wanted to introduce myself but, at the time, I wasn't myself.
    A huge sailor hat gripped my head and I couldn't lift a teacup

With this ghastly hook. "If it won't ruin the afternoon," I said
    To the waitress, "I'll have some tea and a godforsaken menu."

Homer sat there glaring at me with ferocious, glass-blue eyes.
    His enormous spoon hovered, dripping, halfway to his mouth.

Grandpa had been neglectful but he taught me never to lower
    My gaze. I clenched my one good hand. I could stare forever.

Like prison inmates at lunchtime, I lifted my hook to the light,
    He petted the limp pheasant's head in his sack under the table.

Round Midnight (2)

Hotel sign in Greece:
Clytemnestra's Inn. With Bath.
"Let's get outta here."

Sleeping Lions (2)

Evenings, in the damp grass under the folding table.
   Were you grappling with your loneliness, even then,
Little plastic sword across your lap?
                              The pine trees
   Rustled in the darkness; the Coleman lantern hissed.
I remember: I would tap my father's workboot, then
   One calloused hand would descend, pinching a scrap
Of porkmeat.
                  My mother would skim her bare feet
   Over the grass. Hours, watching the shadows dance
In the turnip garden, listening on the TV to the war
   In Iraq. *But they had made a space for you: a chair,*
A placemat. Once, against the chain-link fence, I sat
   Reading Aeschylus,
                              ignoring their bellowing at me,
Hot blood spurting from Agamemnon's neck. Rain
   Brought us together again: beneath a dripping eve.
Did you believe you'd find something—
                              a little soul—
   Deep within? Mornings, and the gray lambs bleated
In the silence, in the mist. I lay under our dark coats
   In the closet, my mind flittering from empty sleeve
To empty sleeve . . .

Our Pillar

Our son toddled around
In my *Moby-Dick* shirt. Our daughter
Was a bruise-colored blanket
Tumbling from her bed to the floor.
We gathered stuffed animals
In our arms, or we took turns
Spacing out in front of the coffee-
maker. I wrote a poem
About a green ribbon falling
From an egret's beak. One minute
We heard them snoring to
Earth, Wind & Fire; the next
They were squatting on our chests
And gnawing slobberingly
At our fingers. You say,
They meow at sunset, they ooze like mist
Across our floors, they definitely
Have wings. One of them locked us
In the bathroom, the other
Busted us right out. We were
Archaeologists searching for a fabled
Wooden block. Our hands
Glided side by side into the
Darkness under the sofa
Like swans. Remember the end
Of Kafka's "The Bucket Rider"
When the narrator *ascends*
Into the regions of the ice mountains
And is lost forever? Our daughter
Pointed down the hall, to a path
Of floral-print cushions . . .

Notes

Epigraph: The Wayne Shorter quotation is from a 2013 interview (with Laura Sullivan) on NPR's *All Things Considered*.

Page 9: "I'm greener than the grass is green" is a variation of a line of Sappho's fragment 31 ("Paler than summer grass," trans. Sherod Santos) with a not-so-subtle nod to Robert Lowell's "imitation" of the fragment, "Three Letters to Anaktoria," in *Imitations* (1961): "I am greener than the greenest green grass!"

Page 17: "*Art thou a little spirit bearing up a corpse?*" is a corruption of a well-known Epictetus quotation recorded in Marcus Aurelius's *Meditations*: "Thou art a little soul bearing about a corpse," trans. Hastings Crossley.

Page 21: The Jack Halberstam epigraph is a partial definition of "radical passivity," a term coined in his *The Queer Art of Failure* (2011).

Page 23: "Popa's little boxes" refers to Serbian poet Vasko Popa's serial poem, "The Little Box." Also, "*the witness, midwife to my agonies*" is a phrase plucked from Book Four of Virgil's *The Aeneid*, trans. Robert Fagles.

Page 29: The Franz Kafka quotation is a corruption of the final sentence of his short story "The Bucket Rider," trans. Edwin and Willa Muir: "And with that I ascend into the regions of the ice mountains and am lost forever."

Acknowledgements

Props to the editors of the following publications in which these poems, many in slightly different form, first appeared: *Barn Owl Review, Blue Mesa Review, The Common* (online), *CounterPunch, december, Devil's Lake, Free State Review, The Hollins Critic, Momoware, Memorious, The National Poetry Review, Palette Poetry, Poet Lore, Popshot Quarterly* (UK), *The Portland Review, Whiskey Island,* and *Zone 3.*

LAY OUT YOUR UNREST

Printed in Poland
by Amazon Fulfillment
Poland Sp. z o.o., Wrocław

61749235R00020